D0929473

AMERICA'S COLONIZATION AND SETTLEMENT

1585 to 1763

by Marcia Amidon Lusted

HISTORY DIGS

CHERRY LAKE PUBLISHING • ANN ARBOR, MICHIGAN

Published in the United States of America
by Cherry Lake Publishing
Ann Arbor, Michigan
www.cherrylakepublishing.com

Printed in the United States of America
Corporate Graphics Inc
September 2011
CLFA09

Consultants: Brett Barker, associate professor of history, University of Wisconsin–Marathon County; Gail Saunders-Smith, associate professor of literacy, Beeghly College of Education, Youngstown State University

Editorial direction:
Rebecca Rowell

Series design and cover production:
Marie Tupy

Interior production:
Craig Hinton

Photo credits: The British Library/Heritage-Images, cover, 1; Amy Riley/iStockphoto, 5, 19; North Wind Picture Archives, 7, 11, 18, 21; Gina Groves/iStockphoto, 9; Andrew F. Kazmierski/Shutterstock Images, 13; Shutterstock Images, 14; Brianna May/iStockphoto, 16; Red Line Editorial, Inc., 25; Kenneth Wiedemann/iStockphoto, 27; iStockphoto, 30

Library of Congress Cataloging-in-Publication Data
Lüsted, Marcia Amidon.
America's colonization and settlement / by Marcia Amidon Lüsted.
p. cm. – (Language arts explorer. History digs.)
Includes bibliographical references.
ISBN 978-1-61080-194-2 – ISBN 978-1-61080-282-6 (pbk.)
1. United States–History–Colonial period, ca. 1600-1775–Juvenile literature. 2. United States–Social life and customs–To 1775–Juvenile literature. 3. Community life–United States–History–Juvenile literature. 4. City and town life–United States–History–Juvenile literature. I. Title.
E188.L95 2011
973.2–dc22
2011015119

Cherry Lake Publishing would like to acknowledge the work of The Partnership for 21st Century Skills. Please visit www.21stCenturySkills.org for more information.

TABLE OF CONTENTS

Your Mission 4
What You Know 4
Stepping Back in Time 6
Who Was First? 9
Growing Up in Smithtown 12
A Visit to Jamestown 15
Meeting Smithtown's Slaves 17
Boys Have All the Fun 20
Learning a Trade 23
Mission Accomplished! 26
Consider This 26
Glossary 28
Learn More 29
Further Missions 30
Index 31

You are being given a mission. The facts in What You Know will help you accomplish it. Remember the clues from What You Know while you are reading the story. The clues and the story will help you answer the questions at the end of the book. Have fun on this adventure!

YOUR MISSION

Your mission is to learn to think like a historian. What tools do historians use to research the past? What kinds of questions do they ask, and where do they look for answers? On this assignment, your goal is to investigate U.S. history between 1585 and 1763. This was a time when the United States was not a nation but a group of **colonies** that belonged to England. Find out about colonial America. How was life in **colonial** times different from life today? What was life like for children? What types of jobs did people do? What can you learn about the past from **artifacts** of the time? As you read, keep What You Know in mind.

WHAT YOU KNOW

★ There are living history museums that show what life was like in a colonial town in the early eighteenth century.

★ Many types of people lived in colonial towns, including merchants, **apprentices**, **indentured servants**, and slaves.

★ The first English settlement in America that survived was Jamestown. It was located in what is now the state of Virginia. Archaeologists discovered much of what we know about life in Jamestown.

★ Slavery began in the colonies because **plantation** owners wanted workers for their fields.

This is a replica of a traditional Pilgrim settler's home at Plimoth Plantation in Plymouth, Massachusetts.

Use this book to explore history in ways a historian might. Read the following journal to discover what one student learned about this time period during a visit to a living history museum.

Entry 1:
STEPPING BACK IN TIME

My family is on vacation in Virginia. I walk through the gates of Colonial Smithtown with my family and feel as though I have stepped back in time. It's amazing!

Experiencing a Living History Museum

There are horses and carts, and there are people dressed in colonial clothes. They aren't dressed like us. Only other visitors are dressed like us, in modern clothes. Boys are playing on a large green lawn in front of a big white church. The boys are wearing pants with suspenders and funny hats that have three corners. There are some girls in long dresses and white caps, but they aren't running around and playing like the boys.

LIVING HISTORY MUSEUMS

There are many living history museums in the United States. You can visit them to find out more about what life was like in a particular time. They also preserve many important buildings and artifacts from the past. Some people visit these museums to do research. Colonial museums of this type include Jamestown Settlement and Colonial Williamsburg in Virginia and Old Sturbridge Village and Plimoth Plantation in Massachusetts. In the Midwest, many living history museums focus on pioneers from the nineteenth century. Fort Snelling in Minnesota presents life in the 1820s in a frontier military fort. Old World Wisconsin highlights the experiences of immigrant farmers in the late nineteenth century.

Artists often depict scenes from life. This image shows colonists on an old Jamestown street, Virginia Colony, in the 1600s.

There are many buildings. Some of them are more than 300 years old! But there aren't any electrical wires, telephones, cars, or indoor bathrooms! I think it would have been a hard life.

Smithtown seems as big as any regular small town today. The streets aren't paved, though. They are dirt. I see some places where people can tie their horses. Big puffs of dust follow the horses' hooves as they plod along pulling buggies and wagons.

All the buildings at Colonial Smithtown are made of brick or wood and have small windows. The buildings themselves seem small. Most of the houses have a garden and lots of animals. Stray dogs are running everywhere, and cats slip through fences—maybe to avoid the dogs. I hear chickens clucking and cows mooing. I wrinkle my nose because it smells like manure!

History Interpreter

A woman is sitting in front of one of the buildings. She is wearing a fancy dress. I walk over to her as she talks to another visitor. She's pretending to be a woman named Mrs. Smith, the wife of Smithtown's mayor. Mom says these people are called **interpreters**. They answer people's questions and tell them things about Smithtown, its history, and what life is like there. I think it would be fun to do that.

Mrs. Smith is talking about the kinds of things she does every day. She seems to know everything about Smithtown. Pretending to be part of history sounds like more fun than just reading about it in school! I'm eager to find out more. ★

WHO WAS FIRST?

My family is having lunch, and I tell Mom I am confused by what I am learning at Colonial Smithtown. I thought the Pilgrims in Massachusetts were the first English colonists in the Americas. Mom tells me explorers from England and other parts of Europe were here before the Pilgrims. The English settled first at Jamestown in Virginia in 1607.

The Pilgrims traveled to America to start a new life.

THE MAYFLOWER COMPACT

The Mayflower Compact was one of the first instances of self-government in the colonies. The Pilgrims were still loyal to the British monarchy, but they clearly said they would make their own laws. The colonists' desire to rule themselves increased until the Revolutionary War (1775–1783), when the colonies formed the United States of America and became independent from England.

The Pilgrims

The Pilgrims were looking for religious freedom. Most people in England belonged to the Anglican Church. The Pilgrims thought the Anglican Church was too concerned with wealth and fancy worship. The Pilgrims wanted a simple, less worldly church. They wanted to separate themselves from the Anglican Church and worship in their own way. They were called Separatists. But they were not allowed to practice their own religion in England. Some went to the Netherlands to escape **persecution**, but they were unhappy there. The group had heard about America and decided in 1617 to emigrate there. The group returned to England, where it joined other Separatists. And in 1620, the group headed to America to build a colony. The Separatists made the rules for their new settlement before they even landed. The rules were called the Mayflower Compact.

The Pilgrims landed on the coast of Massachusetts and settled Plymouth, which they spelled *Plimoth*. Fishermen, trappers, and explorers from Europe had been there before, but the Pilgrims were the first Europeans to actually settle there. It was a hard place to survive. The soil was rocky and the weather was cold and windy. But the Pilgrims were determined to start farms and grow food to support themselves. They also hoped to one day ship furs, fish, and lumber to England to make money. Their main goal, though, was simply to survive. With the help of American Indians such as members of the Wampanoag tribe, they managed to do just that.

Other groups came to America after the Pilgrims. They traveled from England and other European countries. They started their own settlements. Soon, the settlements combined under English control to make the original colonies. There were 13: New Hampshire, Massachusetts, Rhode Island, Connecticut, New York, New Jersey, Pennsylvania, Delaware, Maryland, Virginia, North Carolina, South Carolina, and Georgia. But Mom says the colonies—and ultimately the United States—really started with Jamestown. That settlement proved America was a good place to live. ★

The Pilgrims struggled to survive after settling in the area that is now Massachusetts. This is how one artist imagined the Pilgrims' experience.

Entry 3: GROWING UP IN SMITHTOWN

I'm back at Colonial Smithtown. It's the second day of our trip, and I want to talk to more interpreters today. I see a girl who looks about my age. She says her name is Meg. Her family is wealthy. Sometimes, she plays the spinet, a kind of piano, in one of the houses. She learned from a music master who came to her house and taught her.

Meg describes what it's like growing up in Smithtown. She tells me all about toys and games that colonial children play. I ask her if she likes acting at Smithtown. She stares at me in confusion. She doesn't seem to know what I'm talking about. Apparently, the interpreters will only act as though it's the eighteenth century.

BECOMING AN INTERPRETER

The costumed interpreters at living history museums go through special training. They learn all about life in their historic community. They learn how to talk and act like people from that time. They learn about their costumes and what chores and activities they'll be doing. They try very hard to stay in character. Visitors can try to get the interpreters to talk about their real, twenty-first century lives, but the interpreters will stick to their historical stories.

Actors in costume at Colonial Williamsburg help visitors understand what life was like for some during this period of U.S. history.

Indentured Servants and Slaves

I ask Meg why her family came to Smithtown. She said her father was a merchant in London. They came to Smithtown because it was a good place to grow tobacco. Her father buys tobacco from farmers and then sells it to people in England.

Meg tells me growing tobacco takes a lot of workers. The farmers use indentured servants who are white. Farmers pay for these servants to come to the colonies from Europe. In exchange, the indentured servants agree to work for five to seven years for free. After those years are done, they will be free.

I learn from Mom that this method of getting workers to tend the farm only worked for a while. Soon, the tobacco farmers needed more workers. They started using enslaved people from Africa. Unlike indentured servants, who would eventually earn their freedom, slaves were slaves forever, and their children would be slaves, too. The colonists believed Africans were not as good as white people because of the color of their skin and their religions. Europeans thought of themselves as more refined than Africans, and this belief went to America with the colonists. The colonists felt this difference made slavery acceptable. Slavery was also appealing for financial reasons. It was cheaper to own slaves than to pay for indentured servants.

Meg says her mother has a family of indentured servants to help in the house. They came from Europe with financial help from Meg's father. According to Meg, the family will have to work for her parents for five years to pay off the cost of traveling here. ★

Entry 4:
A VISIT TO JAMESTOWN

Today, my family is at Jamestown. It was the first English colony in North America that survived. Mom says everyone thought the original James Fort and the settlement had been washed away into the James River. But archaeologists found remains of the fort, including traces of wells, graves, and other buildings. We see exhibits with artifacts the scientists found. The guide tells us the archaeologists have discovered more than 1 million artifacts! Pieces of items such as coins, weapons, pots, and games tell archaeologists what life was like in Jamestown. The scientists even dug up old garbage heaps and found remains of food and bones. The **archaeology** part sounds like fun, but I'm not sure I'd want to dig in garbage!

Roanoke Colony

Our guide tells us there was an English colony even older than Jamestown. Located in present-day North Carolina, it was called

ARCHAEOLOGY

Archaeology is sometimes the only way historians can find out about a settlement or culture that seems to have vanished. Even something like a darkened place in the soil can tell where posts for a building were once placed in the ground. Experts can often tell where pottery or glass shards were made, which gives them clues about inhabitants' homelands or social status. Skeletons can tell scientists what people ate and why they died.

Crosses mark the graves of Jamestown colonists.

Roanoke Colony. It was settled in 1585, more than 20 years before Jamestown. The guide says it didn't last very long, and many of the settlers went back to England.

Another group of settlers came in 1587. It had approximately 115 people, including women and children. But when English ships came back with more supplies in 1590, no one could find any of the Roanoke colonists. All that was left was the word "CROATOAN" carved on a post. The guide explains that some historians think the settlers left for the island of Croatoan, near Cape Hatteras in North Carolina. But no one knows for sure. No signs of them have ever been found. It's still a big mystery. I think it's pretty creepy. ★

Entry 5:
MEETING SMITHTOWN'S SLAVES

Today, we are back at Colonial Smithtown. I want to meet other children to learn more about growing up in Smithtown. I find some children playing the parts of slaves. One boy introduces himself as Jim. He tells me he is a slave. Jim's mother came from Africa on a slave ship. She works in the kitchen of one of the big houses in Smithtown. His father works on a tobacco plantation. Owners of large plantations keep lots of slaves to do the work of growing tobacco and other crops. Jim hardly sees his father.

Jim and I talk for a while. He explains that, though he is a child, he also works. Jim does chores around the house. He and his mother and sister sleep in a loft over the kitchen. Jim explains he will have to work in the fields when he is older. His little sister is learning to work in the laundry washing clothes.

SLAVERY'S LONG HISTORY

Slavery has existed for a very long time. The ancient Greeks and Romans kept slaves. People captured during battles often became slaves. The Portuguese started using Africans as slaves in 1442. During the twentieth century, people were forced to work as slaves in camps such as those of the Nazis during World War II.

Slaves from Africa were introduced to Jamestown in the early 1600s.

From Africa to the Colonies

Jim describes how slavery came to America. Dutch ships brought the first enslaved Africans to Jamestown in 1619. Soon, the colonial farmers wanted more slaves to work in the fields. They couldn't use American Indians because they were more likely to catch diseases from the colonists. Settlers saw Africans as more physically able to do the backbreaking labor needed to create a successful plantation. Some settlers also thought Africans would be less likely to escape because they didn't know the land as well as the American Indians who were native to it.

The settlers began buying slaves from slave traders. Jim explains that slave traders sail to Africa and capture people there, sometimes stealing children from their parents. Sometimes, they buy slaves from African tribes who sell members of other tribes they have captured. Then, the traders pack the slaves tightly into ships with barely enough room to move. Many of the slaves get sick and die during the journey. The ones who survive are sold when the ship reaches America. The slaves spend the rest of their lives working for their masters who buy and sell them as though they are property, not people. I'm glad Jim is really a boy in the twenty-first century and only pretending to be a slave. ★

Entry 6:
BOYS HAVE ALL THE FUN

I've been wandering around Smithtown. I notice something that seems kind of odd. It looks as though only boys are having fun playing outside. I don't see Meg anywhere. I go inside one of the houses and find a girl named Jane who is younger than I am. She is sewing by the fireplace. I ask what she is making. She says it's a sampler. It has all kinds of letters and pictures stitched on it in threads of many colors.

Life for a Colonial Girl

It is pretty hot inside, so I ask Jane why she doesn't go outside to play. Jane says girls aren't supposed to play outside very much in Smithtown. Sometimes, she plays a game called **quoits** outside with other girls. They make rings out of thin rope or twisted branches and

EDUCATING GIRLS

Most girls in colonial America did not attend school. Some did attend dame schools. These were similar to today's nursery schools and were run by women. Here, children learned the alphabet and the New Testament of the Bible. After that, it was considered more important to teach girls how to cook and sew and run a household than to attend school and advance their education. Even today, there are places in Asia and Africa where girls are not allowed to go to school. In those cultures, it is considered more important to educate boys.

Needlework has been a common pastime for centuries.

toss them. What she describes reminds me of horseshoes, a game my grandfather plays. Mostly, the girls are supposed to learn how to sew and keep house. It doesn't sound like much fun to me. Through the window, I can see boys racing down the street, rolling wooden hoops.

Jane tells me she keeps a diary about her life at Smithtown. She shows me an entry:

Today Mother gave me a ***receipt*** *book. It is a fine leather-covered notebook that I will fill with receipts for food and medicine, and making dyes. I am excited to start, and I am glad that Master Turner taught me to write with a clear hand.*

This afternoon it turned stormy, so Mother asked Grace to read aloud to us from the Bible while we sewed. She is doing well for being only six years of age, but I did help her with some of the difficult words. I am nearly done with my sampler, and I am proud of my neat stitches and the beautiful colors of the silk thread.

Then Mother instructed me in making a plain boiled pudding for our dinner. I do not know why I must learn cooking and receipts when we have servants to cook for us. But Mother tells me that even in a household with servants, a young woman needs to know how to do everything herself before she can instruct them.

Entry 7:
LEARNING A TRADE

It's almost time to leave Colonial Smithtown. Before leaving, I meet a boy about my age. His name is Sam. He works in the silversmith's shop. He's an apprentice. He tells me that an apprentice works in a business for free, learning how to do everything required of the business. An apprentice might work for a printer, a rope maker, a candle maker, or any other kind of job. The master, the person who owns the business, feeds the apprentice, gives him a place to live, and also teaches the apprentice how to read and write. When the apprentice is grown up, he can start his own business or keep working for his master.

Being an Apprentice

Sam's job looks interesting. He is keeping a big open fire burning by squeezing air onto it with **bellows**. His master is melting silver over the fire and pouring it into a mold to make silver spoons. Silversmiths make a variety of household goods, including silverware, plates, cups, bowls, and fancy tea sets. They often make

MODERN APPRENTICES

There are still jobs today where people work as apprentices for more experienced masters. Electricians, plumbers, and even engineers often start as apprentices until they know enough about their job to work on their own. However, unlike colonial times, apprentices don't have a master who provides food and lodging, and an apprentice can quit more easily.

these items with silver from coins they have melted down. It's hard to imagine that someone my age would have worked all the time instead of going to school.

Sam says his master is worried about selling enough silver. There are several other silversmiths in Smithtown, and too many of the rich planters are buying their fancy silver and furniture and china from England. So, Sam's master also fixes clocks and repairs broken cups and makes silver teeth. Silver teeth? Those sound uncomfortable!

The Triangular Trade Route

Sam says the colonists are better off selling things such as lumber, fish, and tobacco to England. It is something called a triangular trade route: America sends raw materials to England, England makes things from those materials and sells them to Africa and America, and traders leaving Africa bring slaves to America and sell them. Sam says if you draw these trade routes on a map, they form a triangle, and that's where the name comes from.

Mom finds me just as the sun starts to set. I tell her about the trade route Sam described. She also explains that few, if any, ships actually made the entire triangular trip. Most went back and forth between two ports or areas, while other ships sailed the other sides of the triangle.

It's a lot to take in. Not just the trade route, but being an apprentice, an indentured servant, a slave, a colonial child—all of it. Life in colonial America was so different than my life. It's time to go. I really like Smithtown, but I am glad that I'm able to walk through the gates, hop in the car, and go back to the modern hotel swimming pool. ★

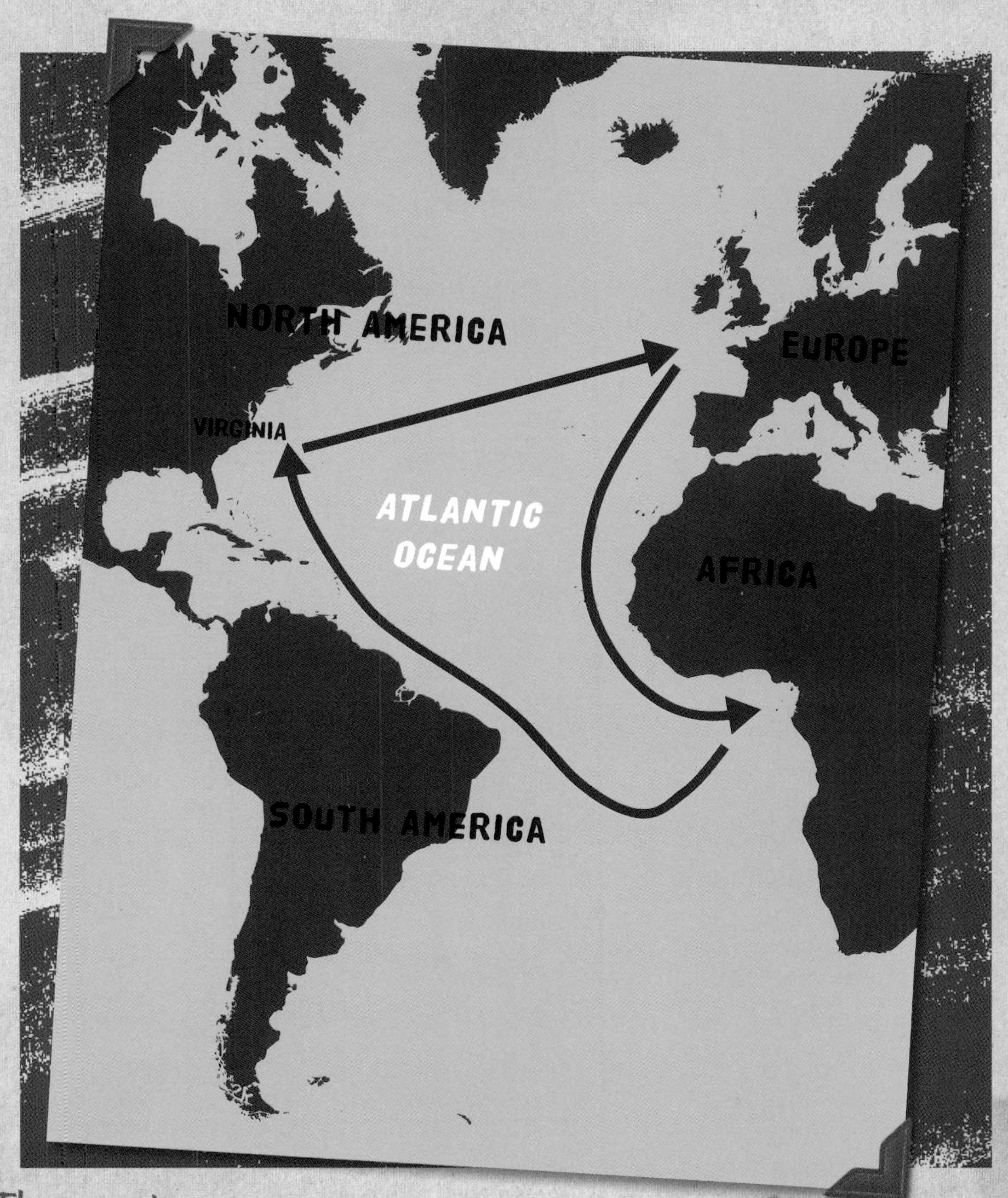

This map shows the triangular trade route that brought Africans to the colonies to work as slaves and goods to England from the colonies.

MISSION ACCOMPLISHED!

Congratulations! You learned a lot about what life was like in a colonial American town. You learned that English settlers came to Jamestown first, and a lot of what we know about them comes from archaeology. You discovered that a colonial town had many different kinds of people. There were merchants, apprentices, indentured servants, and slaves. You know that the settlers needed more workers to help them grow crops that could earn a lot of money, such as tobacco, and they eventually decided to use slaves. You read about the triangular trade route and how it brought slavery to colonial America. And you know more about what children were expected to do during this period of U.S. history. Good job!

CONSIDER THIS

- ★ How did people become apprentices, indentured servants, or slaves in colonial America? Did they have a choice? What if they wanted to do something else?
- ★ Have the same things that made people want to settle in America also helped settle other parts of the world? What makes people want to move to a new place, especially one so far away?
- ★ Imagine what it must have been like to be an apprentice in colonial America. Would you have liked being one? What skill would you like to be able to do? Are you glad you don't have to work as a child, or would you rather work?

You can visit living history museums such as Colonial Williamsburg to learn more about colonial America.

★ If you had the choice, would you become a colonist in a distant land? Why or why not?

apprentice (uh-PREN-tis) a person who is learning a craft or trade by working for a skilled worker

archaeology (ahr-kee-AH-luh-jee) the scientific study of the past using artifacts and other relics

artifact (AHR-tuh-fakt) an object made by people in the past

bellows (BEL-ohz) a tool that is squeezed to pump air

colonial (kuh-LOH-nee-uhl) in U.S. history, having to do with the original 13 colonies that became the United States

colony (KAH-luh-nee) a group of people who settle in a distant land but are still citizens of their original country

indentured servant (in-DENT-churd SUR-vuhnt) a person who has signed a contract to work for someone for a specific amount of time

interpreter (in-TUR-pri-tur) someone who explains the purpose or meaning of something

persecution (pur-suh-KYOO-shuhn) the act of being treated unfairly

plantation (plan-TAY-shuhn) a large farm or estate where crops such as cotton or tobacco are grown

quoits (kwoits) a game where rings of rope or twisted branches are thrown at a stake

receipt (ri-SEET) in colonial times, a recipe

shard (shahrd) a piece of broken glass or pottery, such as those found at an archaeological dig

LEARN MORE

BOOKS

Kostyal, Karen. *1776: A New Look at Revolutionary Williamsburg*. Washington, DC: National Geographic Society, 2009.

Ransom, Candice. *Why Did English Settlers Come to Virginia?: And Other Questions About the Jamestown Settlement.* Minneapolis, MN: Lerner Books, 2011.

Raum, Elizabeth. *The Dreadful, Smelly Colonies: The Disgusting Details About Life in Colonial America*. Minneapolis, MN: Capstone Press, 2010.

WEB SITES

Colonial Williamsburg Kid Zone

http://www.history.org/kids/index.cfm

Virtually explore Colonial Williamsburg, meet colonial people, and check out activities, including games.

Jamestown Settlement Kids' Museum Guides

http://www.historyisfun.org/Kids-Museum-Guides.htm

Check out links to information about life at Jamestown Settlement.

Old Sturbridge Village Kid Zone

http://www.osv.org/kids_zone/

Learn about colonial America through games, puzzles, and information just for kids.

FURTHER MISSIONS

MISSION 1

Imagine you are a modern-day colonist, someone who wants to start a new life in another country. Record your thoughts in a journal. What are the reasons for leaving your old country? Where would you go? What would you do once you arrived? How would you try to fit in with your new country and the people there?

MISSION 2

Many living history museums let kids work as historic interpreters. Is there a museum near you? Find out about opportunities for spending summers there as an interpreter. If there is no living history museum near you, look for volunteer opportunities at local libraries, art or history museums, or historical societies. Offer to start your own interpreter program!

INDEX

Africa, 17, 19, 20, 24
Africans, 14, 17, 19
American Indians, 11, 19
Anglican Church, 10
apprentice, 4, 23, 24, 26
archaeologist, 4, 15
archaeology, 15, 26

clothes, 6, 17
Colonial Williamsburg, 6
colonist, 9, 10, 14, 16, 19, 24, 26
colony, 4, 10, 15
Croatoan, 16

education, 20
England, 4, 9, 10, 11, 14, 16, 24

indentured servant, 4, 14, 24, 26
interpreter, 8, 12

James Fort, 15
James River, 15
Jamestown, 4, 6, 9, 11, 15, 16, 19, 26

living history museum, 4, 5, 6, 12

Massachusetts, 6, 9, 10, 11
Mayflower Compact, 10

Old Sturbridge Village, 6
Old World Wisconsin, 6
original colonies, 11

Pilgrim, 9, 10–11
plantation, 4, 6, 17, 19
Plimoth Plantation, 6
Plymouth, 10

quoits, 20, 22

Roanoke Colony, 15–16

sampler, 20, 22
Separatists, 10
silversmith, 23–24
slavery, 4, 14, 17, 26

tobacco, 14, 17, 24, 26
triangular trade route, 24, 26

Virginia, 4, 6, 9, 11

ABOUT THE AUTHOR

Marcia Amidon Lusted is the author of more than 50 books and hundreds of magazine articles for kids. She is also an assistant editor for the children's history magazine *Cobblestone*. She lives in New Hampshire with her family.

ABOUT THE CONSULTANTS

Brett Barker is an associate professor of history at the University of Wisconsin–Marathon County in Wausau. He received his PhD in history from the University of Wisconsin–Madison and his MA and BA in history from Ohio State University. He has worked with K–12 teachers in two Teaching American History grants.

Gail Saunders-Smith is a former classroom teacher and Reading Recovery teacher leader. Currently, she teaches literacy courses at Youngstown State University in Ohio. Gail is the author of many books for children and three professional books for teachers.